# Do You KNOW?™

## THE BOSTON RED SOX

Test your expertise with these fastball questions (and a few curves) about your favorite team's hurlers, sluggers, stats and most memorable moments

*Guy Robinson*

W9-DDJ-475

SOURCEBOOKS, INC.®
NAPERVILLE, ILLINOIS

Published by Sourcebooks, Inc.
P.O. Box 4410, Naperville, Illinois 60567-4410
(630) 961-3900
Fax: (630) 961-2168
www.sourcebooks.com

ISBN-10: 1-4022-1419-7
ISBN-13: 978-1-4022-1419-6

**R**ed Sox Nation is a world overflowing with stuff to remember. But the names, scores, and records are just part of the story. There are also the legends and magic moments, the great feats at the plate and on the mound, and the spectacular catches that you just hadda be there to see. And don't forget the shameful errors, odd characters, strange happenings on and off the field, and all the remarkable things BoSox people have done and said. All this, and more, is fodder for a lively little quiz book. So here it is.

This test reaches back to the beginning and runs the breadth and depth of Sox history and lore right up to the present. Some of the answers will jump quickly to mind, but others may knock you as flat as if you've chased a fly ball right into the Green Monster, and send you to the record books, the team histories, and the websites to learn more. And some may prompt you to test other Red Sox fans; what's more satisfying than spreading around a nugget of Soxiana that isn't widely known?

So here are 100 questions. Count ten points for each correct answer. Where a question has more than one part, you'll be told how to divide the credit. Here and there you'll find a chance to earn bonus points, so it's theoretically possible to score more than 1,000. (But you won't!)

Figure your performance this way:

| | |
|---|---|
| Above 900: | **Spectacular!** |
| 700–899: | A very solid showing |
| 500–699: | Nothing to be ashamed of |
| Below 500: | Told you it was tough |

1. Which was *not* a nickname for Ted Williams?

    a. "The Splendid Splinter"
    b. "Teddy Ballgame"
    c. "The Batmeister"
    d. "The Thumper"
    e. "The Kid"

2. On July 29, 2003, Bill Mueller became the fourth Red Sox batter to knock out a pair of grand slams in a single game—more than any other team. Mueller's feat was uncommon enough, but what made it even rarer? (Bonus: five points apiece for the names of the other three BoSox players who've hit a pair.)

    _____

3. What station on the Green Line of the T is closest to Fenway Park?

    _____

4. What did Bill Buckner say after letting Mookie Wilson's roller slip through his legs in Game 6 of the '86 World Series?

    a. "Must've hit a pebble or something. Right?"
    b. "That was the single worst moment of my life, and I'll bet no one will ever let me forget it."
    c. "If God had wanted it to be the other way around, that's how it would have been."
    d. "Look, guys, I'm sorry but this is really not something I want to discuss, all right?"

5. Before the "Impossible Dream" season, 1967, how many consecutive losing seasons had Red Sox fans endured?

    a. 5                    c. 8
    b. 7                    d. 12

6. In the last month of that '67 season, first-place Boston battled three challengers for the top spot in the American League. For your ten points, you must name all three.

_____

_____

_____

7. What did Johnny Damon, Lenny DiNardo, and Kevin Youkilis do for Bronson Arroyo while all four were with the Sox? (Hint: It was off the field, and it was something dirty.)

_____

8. In the famous sixth game of the '75 World Series against favored Cincinnati, Carlton Fisk stood by home plate and used both hands to wave his high fly ball into the left field foul pole for a game-winning home run. In what inning?

_____

9. Earlier in that same game, with two men on, two outs, and the Reds up 6-3 in the bottom of the eighth, what Boston batter homered to tie the game? (Five bonus points if you name the Reds pitcher he faced in that inning.)

_____

10. You may have heard of one of my brothers, who played for years with another American League club, or another of my brothers, who played for the Pirates and other National League teams. I, myself, was a longtime Red Sox center fielder. Who was I? (Ten bonus points if you can give at least two lines of the jingle Bostonians used to sing about me.)

_____

11. The reporter asks, "Where do the Sox rank in importance in your life?" The answer: "I say the Red Sox...sex...and breathing." Who gives that answer? (Hint: "Live, from New York...!")

_____

12. "Boston Red Sox, Established _____." What year?

    a. 1876
    b. 1901
    c. 1907
    d. 1908

13. The Sox were last in either league to integrate, hiring second baseman Pumpsie Green in 1959. What was Pumpsie Green's real first name?

    a. Paul
    b. Morton
    c. Elijah
    d. Pumpsie

14. With what broadcast veteran was Joe Castiglione first teamed to announce BoSox games?

_____

15. Moe Berg, the catcher, spent his final playing days, in the '30s, with the Red Sox. Just before he died, in 1972, his last words reportedly were:

    a. "You know, I always wanted to be a pitcher."
    b. "I think them Sox could go all the way this year."
    c. "They call that Fisk a catcher? Hah!"
    d. "How did the Mets do today?"

16. One day, during a game at Fenway, utility man Ed Jurak used his glove to catch something in the infield that wasn't a ball. What was it?

_____

17. Roger Clemens racked up 20-strikeout games a decade apart, in 1986 and 1996. Five points apiece for naming the teams that got the Rocket treatment.

_____

18. For five points, name the street behind the Green Monster; for five more, on what street adjacent to Fenway will you find the players' parking lot?

_____

_____

19. Which event upstaged the opening of Fenway Park in Boston newspapers?

    a. The sinking of the *Titanic*
    b. The sinking of the *Lusitania*
    c. The inauguration of President
       Woodrow Wilson
    d. The Johnson-Jeffries
       heavyweight boxing match

20. What's gehrig38?

_____

_____

21. Shortstop Luis Aparicio joined the Red Sox in 1971. Coming from what team?

_____

22. What Sox slugger got the last major league hit yielded by Satchel Paige? (In the old guy's final appearance, representing the Kansas City Athletics, he was, according to best guesses, 59 or 60.)

_____

23. BoSox math:

| | |
|---|---|
| Start with Ted's '41 BA, no decimal: | _____ |
| − longest # of yrs b/n Sox world titles: | _____ |
| ÷ Cronin's uniform #: | _____ |
| − yrs Babe Ruth played for Sox: | _____ |
| ÷ Lee or Piersall uniform #: | _____ |
| = What's the result? | _____ |

24. Who was Helen Robinson to Red Sox Nation?

    a. Jackie Robinson's widow, who became a great Red Sox fan after he died
    b. Switchboard operator who knitted sweaters for players in military service
    c. Female outfielder who played two games dressed as a man in 1902
    d. First Fenway organist and composer of "Take Me Out to the Ballgame"

25. In the ninth inning of Game 6 of the 1975 World Series, with bases loaded, Denny Doyle, running when he shouldn't have, was thrown out at the plate. Why did he say he tried for the plate? (Hint: He claimed a mishearing.)

_____

26. What did Wade Boggs, Roger Clemens, and Johnny Damon have in common?

_____

27. What did Jack Fisher give to Ted Williams?

_____

**28. And after that, what did Ted do for the cheering fans?**

    a. Stood by the dugout, bowing and waving
       for five minutes
    b. Saluted the crowd and disappeared
    c. Made an obscene gesture
    d. Stayed out of sight

**29. Fenway Park is:**

    a. the oldest active major
       league ballpark
    b. second oldest
    c. third oldest
    d. not in the running to be
       ranked

**30. What's the next number in this series: 1, 4, 8, 9, _____?**

**31. In what year did Yaz win the Triple Crown?**

_____

**32. Yaz, by the way, had at least 100 hits in every season he played save for one: 1981. That year he had just 83. Why?**

_____

**33. As a third baseman, I once registered hits in 12 consecutive at-bats, the last eight of them in a double-header. I also managed the Sox for a time. But whatever I may have accomplished, I'm remembered mostly for some racist statements, and for having been jailed for a drunk driving episode that killed a highway worker and injured three more. Who was I?**

_____

34. In the game in which Alex Rodriguez knocked the ball out of Bronson Arroyo's glove, what happened to A-Rod?

    a. He was called out
    b. He was called safe at first base
    c. The pitch was replayed
    d. Arroyo decked him

35. And how about the game in which catcher Jason Varitek shoved A-Rod in the face with his mitt hand? What happened?

    a. Varitek was ejected from the game; A-Rod wasn't
    b. Varitek was ejected; A-Rod too
    c. A-Rod was ejected; Varitek wasn't
    d. They both stayed

36. In 1984, all three starting Sox outfielders topped 100 RBIs. With their initials as hints, name them.

    LF: J_____ R _____

    CF: T_____ A _____

    RF: D_____ E _____

37. I pitched my way to 511 wins during a 22-year career, 192 of them in eight years with the Boston franchise. There's a big award named after me. Who was I?

    _____

38. In 1969 Rico Petrocelli hit 40 home runs. How many did he have in his entire 13-year career, all spent with the Sox?

    a. 80
    b. 210
    c. 350
    d. 450

39. Harry Frazee, the owner who sold Babe Ruth to the Yankees, was also:

    a. a Broadway producer
    b. a shoe manufacturer
    c. a vaudeville tap dancer
    d. a barber

40. What was the score of the "Shuttle Series"?

_____

41. What's different about grandstand sections 32 and 33 at Fenway? (Hint: Sam is nowhere to be found.)

_____

42. What did John Valentin do to the Mariners on July 8, 1994?

_____

43. Who was the Red Sox player who delivered the first home run ever hit by a designated hitter, three days after the American League's DH rule went into effect, in 1973?

_____

44. "I have nothing to be ashamed of. He hit 60 others, didn't he?" Who said it?

_____

45. How do citizens of Red Sox Nation refer to the White Sox?

    a. The Pale Stockings
    b. The Windy Sox
    c. The Midwestern Hosiery
    d. The Other Sox

46. To still-seething Red Sox fans, what do Bucky Dent and Aaron Boone have in common? (Hint: Don't expect to read *all* the details here. This is a family book.)

_____

47. And what Boston pitchers are forever associated with the aforementioned Dent and Boone? Five points apiece:

_____

48. Match the players with their nicknames. Two points each.

    a. "Spaceman"
    b. "Monster"
    c. "Pudge"
    d. "Big Papi"
    e. "The Little Professor"

    f. Dick Radatz
    g. David Ortiz
    h. Bill Lee
    i. Dom DiMaggio
    j. Carlton Fisk

49. Five more players, five more nicknames. Two points each again.

    a. "Gator"
    b. "Chicken Man"
    c. "Dewey"
    d. "The Grey Eagle"
    e. "Hit Dog"

    f. Wade Boggs
    g. Dwight Evans
    h. Tris Speaker
    i. Mo Vaughn
    j. Mike Greenwell

50. In Game 6 of the '86 World Series, just before the fatal Mookie-to-Buckner ground ball, a wild pitch to Mookie by Sox right-hander _____ allowed the tying run to score. (Ten bonus points: who scored on that pitch?)

51. What Neil Diamond song is played before the home half of every eighth inning at Fenway Park?

_____

52. The 1999 ALCS game known as "The Duel" pitted Red Sox right-hander _____ _____against Roger Clemens, in the turncoat's first year as a Yankee.

53. What's the proper response to "Where is Roger?"

_____

54. Who generally is credited for popularizing the name "Pesky's Pole" referring to the right field foul pole at Fenway Park?

a. Joe McCarthy
b. Walt Dropo
c. Mel Parnell
d. Pesky himself

55. Who beaned Tony C.?

_____

56. Name the autobiography and the 1957 movie that tell the Jimmy Piersall story: _____ _____
_____. (Ten bonus points who starred in the movie?)

57. Which Red Sox outfielder explained his playing in close, almost like a fifth infielder, by saying: "I learned early that I could save more games by cutting off some of those singles than I could lose by having an occasional extra base hit go over my head."

    a. Carlos Quintana
    b. Dwight Evans
    c. Joe DiMaggio
    d. Tris Speaker

58. What Sox catcher, upon being traded to the Indians in 1960, chose to retire rather than go to Cleveland? (Hint: He once scored three times in one inning.)

_____

59. What does David Ortiz have tattooed on his right bicep?

_____

60. What southpaw pitcher known as "Sweet Music" sustained an elbow injury at Fenway Park early in the 1994 season and never again pitched for the Sox?

_____

61. I sometimes talked about things like extraterrestrial life, pyramid power, and Zero Population Growth. I took ginseng before I pitched and talked about sprinkling marijuana into my buckwheat pancakes. When I wrote the story of my life in baseball, I titled it _The Wrong Stuff_. So I must be the offspeed specialist named:

_____

62. Which of these items *can't* you find at the food stands in or around Fenway Park?

    a. Fenway Frank
    b. Legal Sea Foods clam chowder
    c. Luis Tiant Cuban sandwich
    d. Boston Cream Pie on a stick
    e. Remdawg

63. Which Sox catcher and later TV sportscaster was the last player in the major leagues to bat without a helmet? (Five extra points: Why?)

_____

64. On two memorable days in 1950, the Red Sox participated in slugfests ending in scores of 20-4 and a record setting 29-4. Yes, the Sox won both. Against whom?

_____

65. In my first major league game, as a 21-year-old rookie, I took on the Yankees at their stadium. I was within one strike of a no-hitter when Elston Howard singled to right-center field. Oh, well. We did win the game, 3-0, but my career fizzled not long after. My initials are B.R. Who am I?

B_____

R_____

66. Which is older, BDD or SoSH?

_____

67. Curt Schilling delivered for the Sox in the '04 World Series despite an injury to his:

    a. left ankle
    b. right ankle
    c. left heel
    d. right heel

68. What happened to Schilling's red sock from that Series?

    a. It was sold on eBay
    b. It was burned and the ashes buried
    c. It was laundered three times and finally discarded
    d. It went on display at the Baseball Hall of Fame

69. The huge Citgo sign beyond left field at Fenway says:

    a. "CITGO"
    b. "CITGO MOTOR OIL"
    c. "CITGO PETROLEUM CORP."
    d. "CITGO ❤ THE RED SOX"

70. Mel Almada, a left-handed outfielder who broke into the big leagues with the Red Sox in 1933, was the first major leaguer born in

_____

71. Can you name all nine Red Sox managers of the last quarter of the 20th century? Here, in *reverse* order, is a list of their initials. One point for each of the first eight you get, two for the ninth.

D.J.: _____

D.Z.: _____

J.P.: _____

R.H.: _____

J.McN.: _____

J.M.: _____

B.H.: _____

K.K.: _____

J.W.: _____

72. Speaking of initials, whose appear in Morse code on the Fenway Park scoreboard?

_____

73. In 1993, the Red Sox moved their spring training base from

_____
to _____.
(Five points each.)

74. Bill Lee is to eephus as Tim Wakefield is to

_____

75. I was a first baseman whose hitting was solid but my fielding left something to be desired. The story is told that during one game, when a candy bar wrapper blew onto the field, I neatly scooped it up...and got a standing ovation. Who am I?

_____

76. Although I never played beyond the minor leagues, I was with the Red Sox for 65 years, until just before I died in 2001. I managed Boston farm squads and coached, served as acting manager, and coordinated spring training programs for the Red Sox team itself. Folks called me "Pop." Who was I?

_____

77. In 1997 every major league team retired No. 42 to honor the memory of Jackie Robinson. Under a grandfather clause, what BoSox first baseman was allowed to continue to wear the number—with the Sox, the Angels, and finally the Mets—until he retired in 2003?

_____

78. Who preceded the answer to the previous question as starting first baseman for the Sox?

_____

79. Teddy Ballgame quote: "All I want out of life is that when I walk down the street, folks will say, 'There goes the _____

_____  _____  _____  _____.'"

80. "I apologize to the fans of the Red Sox, the people of New England, and baseball fans throughout the world. It was an instant, reflexive reaction that I regret. I appreciate the passion our fans have for baseball in Boston; all of us depend on them and their support. I am very sorry." OK, we get the point: He's sorry. Who said it, and why was he so repentant?

_____

_____

81. "I've seen Nolan Ryan at his finest and Roger Clemens at his finest, and _____ _____ 's control is better than either one." That was American League umpire Larry McCoy speaking about whom?

82. "_____ _____ could hit me at midnight with the lights out." Thus spake Lefty Gomez about a power-hitting first baseman who spent several years of a long career with the Red Sox. Who?

83. Kevin Youkilis: "Cowboy _____!"

84. What former major league shortstop runs a baseball school in Delray Beach, Florida, with facilities that include a full-size replica of Fenway Park, complete with a Green Monster and all?

_____

85. At Fenway Park on June 9, 1946, Ted Williams landed a home run ball in section 42, row 37, seat 21. What's odd about that seat today? (Twenty bonus points: Can you name the fan who was sitting in the seat on that day? Some diehards can.)

_____

86. Fifty-five years later, Manny Ramirez hit a booming home run that was officially estimated at 501 feet. Why?

_____

87. Every member of the Fenway Faithful recalls in excruciating detail the day the Curse was broken: October 27, 2004. But quick—what day of the week was it?

_____

88. "Red Sox fans have longed to hear it: the Boston Red Sox are world champions!" Who said it?

   a. Joe Buck
   b. Tim McCarver
   c. Joe Castiglione
   d. Terry Francona

89. For five points apiece, what was Fred Lynn's rookie year, and what two awards did he win that year?

_____

_____

90. Left fielder Mike Greenwell finished second in the MVP voting for 1988, with a .325 BA, 22 HRs, and 119 RBIs. The award was taken by a player who later spent some time with the Red Sox, and who also wrote a book admitting that he had used steroids during some of his playing years. Who?

_____

91. For five points apiece, identify the former Red Sox sportscaster who was likely to call a home run this way:

   a. "Swing and a drive! Way back! Wa-ay back! HOME RUN!"
     J_____ T_____

   b. "Way up, and gone! Mercy!"
     N_____ M_____

92. My old man was Red Sox general manager. He picked me out of the draft and I played with the team for five seasons in the '80s. I was a catcher, but then, so was Rich Gedman at the time, so I didn't see a lot of action. Who am I?

_____

93. What former Red Sox shortstop saved two women who had fallen into Boston Harbor? (Hint: He once hit two grand slams in a single game.)

_____

94. Can you name the Cleveland right fielder who robbed pinch hitter Dick Williams of a home run in 1963 with a show-stopping leap over the wall and into the bullpen? (Hint: A.L.)

_____

95. Luis Aparicio was a fine fielder and a master of the stolen base, but one time his footwork failed him—during the close race at the end of the '72 season when he messed up a Red Sox rally late in the penultimate game of the season, against Detroit. Rounding third, he slipped and fell, headed back to third, and ran into another base runner, who was coming in from second. The runner was tagged out, the Sox lost, and they missed the playoffs by half a game. Who was the other runner?

_____

96. What denomination is the 2001 United States postage stamp that carries a vintage photo of Fenway Park?

   a. 17¢
   b. 21¢
   c. 31¢
   d. 34¢

97. Trot Nixon—an original Dirt Dog, with the scrappy style and the original filthy cap. "Trot" is a shortened form of his middle name, Trotman. What's his first name?

_____

98. What did Nomar Garciaparra, Scott Fletcher, and Pinky Higgins have in common?

_____

**99. Which feature has *never* been seen on the Green Monster?**

    a. A ladder
    b. A garage door
    c. A time zone clock
    d. Advertisements

**100. "What do the Red Sox and lawn chairs have in common?" What's the punchline, no longer valid, to that old joke?**

" _____

_____."

# ANSWERS

1. c.

2. A switch-hitter, he knocked one from each side of the plate (bonus: Jim Tabor in 1939, Rudy York in 1946, Nomar Garciaparra in 1999)

3. Kenmore

4. c.

5. c.

6. Chicago White Sox, Minnesota Twins, Detroit Tigers

7. They backed him in performing "Dirty Water" on his debut rock album, *Covering the Bases*

8. 12th

9. Pinch hitter Bernie Carbo (bonus: Rawly Eastwick)

10. Dom DiMaggio, brother of Joe and Vince (bonus: "*Who hits the ball and makes it go? Dominick DiMaggio. Who runs the bases fast, not slow? Dominick DiMaggio. Who's better than his brother Joe? Dominick…*")

11. Jimmy Fallon as Sox superfan Ben Wrightman in *Fever Pitch*, the 2004 movie with Drew Barrymore and several Red Sox players as themselves

12. b. (as the Americans)

13. c.

14. Ken Coleman

15. d.

16. A rat

17. Seattle Mariners on April 29, 1986, at Boston; Detroit Tigers on September 19, 1996, at Detroit

18. Lansdowne Street, Van Ness Street

19. a.

20. The screen name used by Curt Schilling on the website Sons of Sam Horn

21. The Chicago White Sox

22. Carl Yastrzemski got the only hit off Paige, a double

23. $406 - 86 \div 4 - 6 \div 37 = 2$

24. b.

25. He said he heard Don Zimmer's shouts of "No! No! No!" as "Go! Go! Go!"

26. Each played for the Yankees after leaving Boston

27. The Baltimore right-hander delivered the ball that became the 420-foot four-bagger that ended the Splinter's playing days—his last AB, his 29th HR of the year (1960), his 521st in a 19-season career

28. d. (as John Updike wrote of the event: "Gods do not answer letters")

29. a.

30. Next is 27 (Red Sox uniform numbers that have been retired: Bobby Doerr's 1, Joe Cronin's 4, Yaz's 8, Ted's 9, and Fisk's 27)

31. 1967

32. A players' strike shortened the season; he played in just 91 games that year

33. Pinky Higgins

34. a. (with riot police standing by)

35. b.

36. LF Jim Rice (122 RBIs), CF Tony Armas (123), RF Dwight Evans (104)

37. Cy Young

38. b.

39. a.

40. In the 1986 World Series, between the Sox of Boston and the Mets of New York, named for the Eastern and Pan Am airline shuttles between the two cities, it was Mets 4-3

41. No alcohol allowed (thus no Sam Adams)

42. He turned an unassisted triple play

43. Orlando Cepeda, off Yankee reliever Sparky Lyle on April 8, 1973

44. Right-hander Tracy Stallard, after serving home run No. 61 to Roger Maris

45. d.

46. Because of their dramatic home runs for the Yankees at just the wrong times, Sox fans have bestowed upon both the middle name "Bleeping"; Bucky Bleeping Dent's homer was in the '78 AL East playoffs, Aaron Bleeping Boone's was in the '03 AL Championship Series

47. Mike Torrez served Dent, Tim Wakefield to Boone

48. a.-h., b.-f., c.-j., d.-g., e.-i.

49. a.-j., b.-f., c.-g., d.-h., e.-i.

50. "The Steamer," Bob Stanley (bonus: Kevin Mitchell)

51. "Sweet Caroline"

52. Pedro Martinez

53. "In the shower!"

54. c.

55. California Angels pitcher Jack Hamilton hit Tony Conigliaro in the face with a pitch on August 8, 1967

56. *Fear Strikes Out* (bonus: Anthony Perkins)

57. d.

58. Sammy White

59. A portrait of his mother, who died in a car crash in 2002

60. Frank Viola

61. Bill Lee

62. d.

63. Bob Montgomery (bonus: when batting helmets were mandated, in 1971, he opted to accept a grandfather exemption, batting instead with just a plastic wafer insert in his cap until he retired in 1979)

64. The St. Louis Browns

65. Billy Rohr

66. The Red Sox fan website Sons of Sam Horn was founded in 1998; the Boston Dirt Dogs site was founded in 2001

67. b.

68. d.

69. a.

70. Mexico (although he was raised in California)

71. Darrell Johnson, Don Zimmer, Johnny Pesky, Ralph Houk, John McNamara, Joe Morgan, Butch Hobson, Kevin Kennedy, Jimy Williams

72. Dots and dashes representing the initials of former owners Thomas A. Yawkey and his wife, Jean R. Yawkey, run vertically down the scoreboard between the columns of out-of-town American League scores

73. Winter Haven to Fort Myers (both in Florida)

74. Knuckleball

75. "Dr. Strangeglove," Dick Stuart

76. Eddie Popowski

77. Mo Vaughn

78. Carlos Quintana

79. "…greatest hitter who ever lived."

80. Byung-Hyun Kim, the pitcher who caused a fuss by responding to fans who booed him at Fenway with a single up-raised finger

81. Pedro Martinez

82. Jimmie Foxx

83. "…up!"

84. Bucky Dent

85. Unlike all the other green seats, this one is red (bonus: Joseph A. Boucher)

86. That's management's respectful nod to Williams, whose red-seat blast was recorded as having traveled 502 feet

87. Wednesday

88. a.

89. 1975; Rookie of the Year and Most Valuable Player

90. José Canseco

91. a. Jerry Trupiano, b. Ned Martin

92. Marc Sullivan (son of former G.M. Haywood Sullivan)

93. Nomar Garciaparra

94. Al Luplow

95. Carl Yastrzemski

96. d.

97. Christopher

98. Their uniform number: 5

99. c.

100. "They both fold and wind up in the cellar right after Labor Day"